The Ancient and Healing Art of

Chinese Herbalism

Published by Ulysses Press, P.O. Box
3440 Berkeley, CA 94703-3440

ISBN 1-56975-139-0

Library of Congress Catalog Card
Number: 98-84045

Distributed in the United States by
Publishers Group West and in Canada by
Raincoast books

First published in Great Britain in 1998
by Hamlyn, an imprint of Reed Consumer
Books Limited

Printed and bound in China

The Ancient and Healing Art of

Chinese Herbalism

Anna Selby

Ulysses Press

Contents

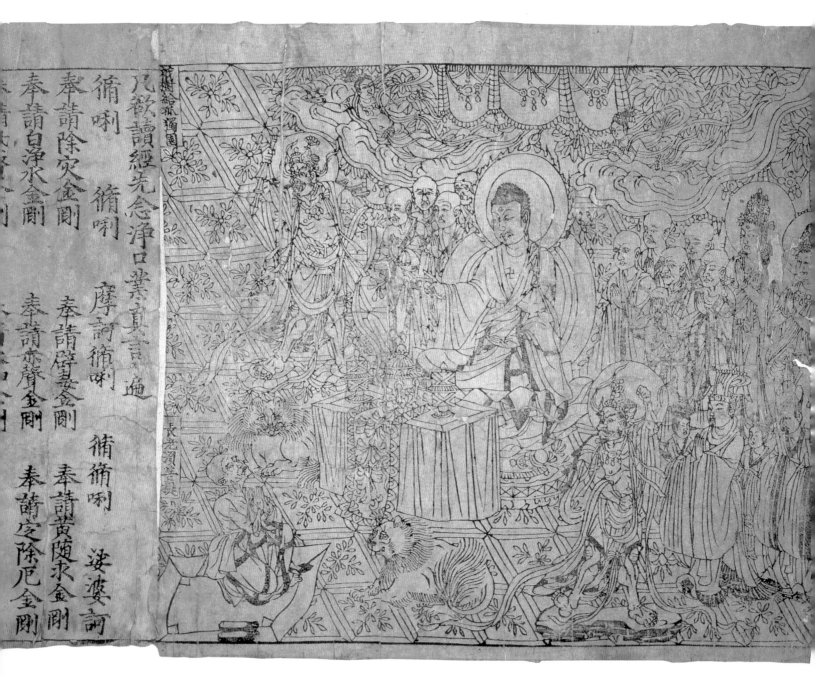

Buddhism is one of the oldest and most important influences on Chinese thought. This frontispiece from the world's earliest printed book – the Diamond Sutra, Dunhuang 868AD – shows the Buddha teaching his aged disciple, Subhuti.

Introduction

Nature cures the disease, the doctor collects the fee.

Chinese proverb

— Ancient China seems as mysterious and unfathomable to the Western world as the dark side of the moon, removed by vast differences of time and space. Yet the Ancient Chinese were responsible for such diverse inventions as silk, paper, gunpowder and the navigational compass, all of which were rapidly absorbed into the Western way of life. In tandem with these developments, China was also devising an extraordinarily complex and complete system of medicine, a process that has continued for thousands of years and that is now gaining the increasing interest of the West.

— Modern Western medicine is rooted in science, with its efficacy proven by controlled tests. Traditional Chinese medicine is quite different. It is based on a vast body of empirical knowledge, gathered over the centuries by the simple method of experiment, experience and observation.

— The underlying philosophies and principles of Chinese medicine vary considerably from our own. Holistic in character, all Chinese medicine aims to cure the fundamental cause of an ailment, rather than merely relieving its symptoms. A Chinese physician does not treat, say, a headache. He looks for the cause of the problem and treats that. So, instead of prescribing a painkiller, he may offer a remedy for anything from liver congestion to emotional stress.

— The science behind the remedies — just as the science behind the invention of gunpowder — was certainly not understood at the time they were first formulated. But clinical experience has shown that they work. Even Western medicine routinely extracts modern drugs from herbs used over centuries by the Chinese. For example, digitalis, extracted from the foxglove plant, is used in Western medicine to treat heart conditions. However, there is growing evidence to suggest that it is often the whole, unrefined plant — as utilized by traditional Chinese medical practitioners — that may be more effective than a particular substance extracted from it and used in isolation.

— Despite the vast body of testimony to the efficacy of Chinese medicine, there is still a great deal of research needed if we are ever to understand, in scientific terms, exactly how this type of medicine works. Once this has been achieved, we may be forced to re-evaluate our own understanding of science itself.

Achieving a Balance

- The Chinese concept of health is one in which the entire system – including both body and mind – is in a state of balance. This balance is the Chinese ideal and the state towards which traditional medicine strives.

- It is fundamental to Chinese philosophy that all life is in a state of constant change. This is true as much of the world around us as it is of our own bodies and emotions. Good health, say the Chinese, can be restored only with balance and harmony. But, influenced from both within and without, our body and mind's balance is constantly being upset, leaving us vulnerable to all manner of ailments.

- On this foundation rests the whole of Chinese medicine. It has evolved into a complete discipline, dealing with physiology, pathology, diagnosis and, most importantly, prevention. Many patients go to a Chinese doctor with nothing more than a vague feeling of being 'not quite well'. This can be used as the basis of a detailed diagnosis to discover the real, underlying problem before it has fully developed. This approach is as old as Chinese medicine itself and was recorded by one 7th-century physician thus: Superior treatment consists of dealing with an illness before it appears, mediocre treatment consists of curing an illness on the point of revealing itself, inferior treatment consists of curing the illness once it has manifested itself.

Yin and Yang

- The notion of balance is symbolized by yin and yang, the two forces contained within the circle of life. Literally, they represent the sunny (yang) and dark (yin) sides of a mountain. According to the Emperor Fu Hsi, who first formulated the concept, the world and all life within it contains this pair of opposites and only when they are in equal balance is life itself in harmony.

- Yang is a positive, active state that is associated with masculinity. It is heat, light, vigour, day, Summer. Yin is a negative, passive state, associated with femininity. It is cold, dark, still, night, Winter.

- Yin and yang are opposing forces, but at the same time they are also mutually dependent. Nature constantly moves between the two, as night follows day and Winter follows Summer. Neither yin nor yang have meaning or existence without the other. Their relationship is a dynamic one, continually moving from imbalance, when one side is dominant, to rebalance and then imbalance again when the opposite side is the stronger.

- Opposing and unifying, yin and yang represent the universal law of heaven and earth.

How the snow contends with the plum blossoms!
Neither will ever own itself vanquished.
The poet lays down his pen and scarcely knows
In whose favour he should decide.
But whereas snow excels with its white colour,
Plum blossoms carry the day with their sweet perfume.
Without snow, plum blossoms seem spiritless;
Without poetry, people are vulgar;
A poem done, new snow, by the end of the day,
Joins with plum blossoms to show the splendour of spring.
Lu Mei-Po (Sung period 960–1127AD)

Above: *The village elders instruct the young about the symbol of yin-yang in this 17th-century painting.*

Left: *A fan painting by Kao Feng-Han (1683–1743) showing bamboo – the yang forces of renewal – growing through the yin, snow-covered landscape.*

Acupuncture

— While all Chinese medicine is governed by the underlying principle of harmony, its practice has diversified into several different forms.

— The best known method of Chinese medicine in the Western world is, without doubt, acupuncture. In prehistoric times, stone 'needles' were used to promote the flow of energy, or Qi, throughout the body, overcoming blockages and strengthening weaknesses, until it was moving smoothly and without hindrance.

— According to the practice of acupuncture, Qi flows through the body via a system of channels known as meridians (called Jing Luo in Chinese and which literally means 'road net'). There is nothing in Western medicine that corresponds directly to the meridians and they are sometimes erroneously thought to be similar to the system of blood vessels (arteries, veins, capillaries) that convey blood around the body. They have also been likened to the central nervous system, and while they are not exactly the same, many acupuncture points do fall close to nerve points identified by Western medicine.

— As the route for the body's vital force, Qi, the meridians embrace all of the body's systems – the central nervous system, the circulatory system, the metabolism and the interchange of Body fluids (see page 46–49).

— There are 12 meridians linked to specific organs or particular body functions, all of which have either a yin or a yang character and a corresponding point on the body into which the needles are inserted.

— Acupuncture uses other processes besides the insertion of needles, including moxibustion and cupping. In moxibustion, a dried herb is burnt over a specific acupuncture point. Cupping uses 'cups' of glass or bamboo that create a vacuum over the skin, drawing it up to remove persistent blockages and encourage the flow of Qi.

— Acupressure is a related discipline in which the pressure of the hands, rather than needles, is used to regulate the Qi. It is thought to have been the forerunner of acupuncture and, while it does not have the same level of success for treating acute ailments as acupuncture does, it is excellent for chronic illnesses. Many people in the West prefer acupressure rather than acupuncture as it does not involve the use of needles.

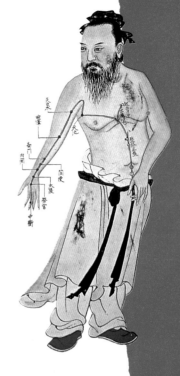

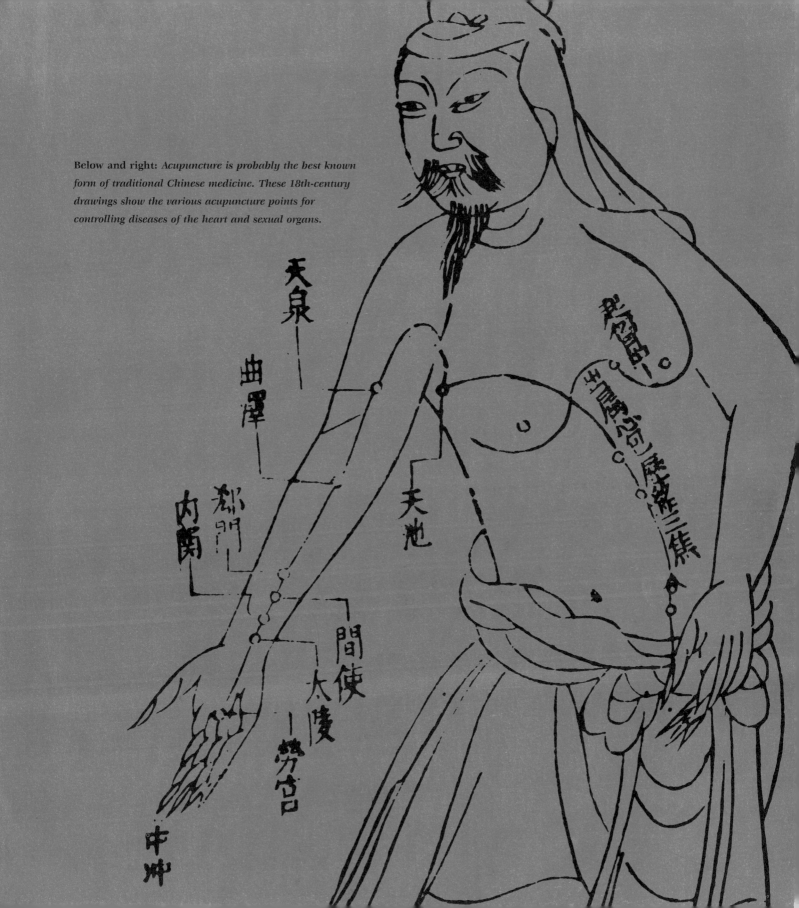

Below and right: *Acupuncture is probably the best known form of traditional Chinese medicine. These 18th-century drawings show the various acupuncture points for controlling diseases of the heart and sexual organs.*

Tai Qi and Qi Gong

— Qi Gong – translated as 'energy cultivation' – is a system of exercises that promote the flow of Qi, creating strong and balanced energy to protect against illness. It focuses particularly on improving the strength and vitality of the three most important of the Five Substances – Qi, Shen and Jing *(see page 46)*. It stills the mind and brings both mind and body into a state of harmony and balance, which in turn acts as a prevention against illness. Qi Gong is believed to be an even older practice than acupuncture and acupressure and it is still very much part of daily Chinese life – the public parks of China are always full of people performing Qi Gong or Tai Qi exercises every morning.

— Qi Gong has exercises for prevention as well as for cures, involving both static postures and sequences of movements not dissimilar to those of Tai Qi, the martial art. Qi Gong also includes a variety of breathing and meditation techniques.

Right: *Album painting of a mountain landscape.*
Far right: *Painting of a tiger attributed to Chen Chu-Chung. The various movements and sequences of Tai Qi and Qi Gong have names that are full of symbolism and imagery. One of the best known of these is 'Embrace Tiger and Return to Mountain' – the tiger being a powerful symbol of yang energy.*

Chinese Nutritional Therapy

Nutritional therapy forms an important element of traditional Chinese medicine and is also based on restoring balance within the body. Very simply, the philosophy is that cooked, slightly warming foods are best, so cold and raw foods (especially frozen ones) should be limited. Fresh and freshly cooked foods are preferred to processed or junk ones and organic foods are best of all.

— So important is nutritional therapy in China that many ailments are believed to be cured by eating the correct foods – in effect, using food as medicine. Traditional Chinese cures include the following:

— Spring onions (scallions) are particularly good for both the stomach and lungs. They are used as a cure for the common cold and also for diarrhoea.

— Turnips act on the lungs and are particularly effective for clearing mucus.

— Carrots are believed by the Chinese to improve vision, particularly in the dark. This concept is also a familiar folk remedy in the West.

— Bananas are taken with breakfast as a cure for constipation.

— Celery is a regulator of unpredictable or very heavy menstrual flow and is also good for relieving headaches related to menstrual problems.

— Ginger should be eaten during pregnancy as it reduces symptoms such as morning sickness and oedema.

Above: *Food, drink and conversation, as enjoyed in China's Yunnan province.*
Left: *Nutrition is central to Chinese medicine. Here, the Kitchen God is shown in the lunar calendar of 1895.*

Early Chinese Medicine

— The history of Chinese medicine goes back at least 4000 years
  – some say 5000. In those distant times, healing was close to
  magic, and superstition was rife. A herb's healing properties
  would often have been discovered accidentally, or by watching
  what animals would instinctively eat to cure themselves when
  they were sick.

— This arcane herbal knowledge was in the hands of shamans.
  They used herbs not only to heal but also to induce trances
  and hallucinations in which they would prophesy or speak
  the words of the gods. In effect, they represented the link
  between heaven and earth.

— As well as through accidental discovery, the properties of
  herbs were also investigated by the shamans. They would
  often try them out on themselves to see what effects they had.
  There are many legends of such shamans. The lore that they
  passed down by word of mouth in that time before the written
  word existed, still forms part of the body of knowledge that
  makes up traditional Chinese medicine today.

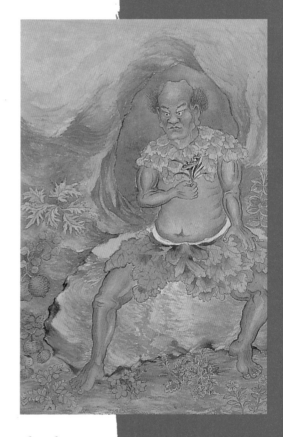

Above: *Seated at the mouth of a mountain cave, is an early god,
possibly a shaman, dressed in traditional garb and holding a branch
with leaves and flowers, whose virtues he is demonstrating.*
Far right: *A detail from an 18th-century emperor's robe showing a
hare pounding the Elixir of Life, within the symbol of the moon.*

黄帝

參贊兩儀
劉與百制德滿輦生澤流萬世

The Legendary Emperors

— Much of the earliest herbal lore is attributed to three legendary emperors – who may also have been shamans.

— The first was Fu Hsi, who is said to have invented the fundamental concept of yin and yang and the striving towards balance that is the law of the whole universe. He is also honoured with the authorship of the *I Ching*, an Ancient Chinese book that can be consulted to obtain advice and answers to questions about the future.

— The most famous of all the herbalist-emperors was Shen Nong, known as the Divine Husbandman and renowned for his testing and tasting of herbs. In the process of his experiments, he was believed to have poisoned himself on a number of occasions but so great was his knowledge of herbs that he always managed to find an antidote. He was thought to have lived around 2500BC or earlier, and was regarded – and possibly worshipped – as the inventor of the plough and of agriculture.

— The third legendary Emperor was Huang Di who was also an inventor – of the first wheeled transport, the planetarium and musical notation. He is believed to have been responsible for divorcing herbalism from its superstitious roots and establishing the role of the physician – as observer, tester and recorder of the effects of herbs.

— All of these three emperors are heavily burdened by legend and tradition and whether they were real emperors – and indeed what constituted an emperor at that time – is open to question, but many legends have their foundation in at least a grain of truth.

Above: The legendary emperors of China were considered to be shamans with supernatural powers. This watercolour is a portrait of Fu Hsi, believed to be the very first Emperor of China.
Left: This 15th-century line drawing is a portrait of the legendary Emperor Huang Di.

Chinese Herbals

— The legendary emperors are known partly from folk stories but, even more importantly, from a handful of classic texts.

— The *Nei Jing*, sometimes known as *Huang Di's Canon of Interior Medicine*, is the most important and influential Chinese herbal ever written. Written around 3000BC, it is in the form of a discussion between the legendary Yellow Emperor and his physician, Chi Bo, and it is still used as a textbook in medical schools in modern China. The book discusses physiology, pathology and therapies and contains the first proper classification of diseases. It also explained for the first time in Chinese medicine how the various organs of the body work and gave advice on exercise and diet.

— It was after the *Nei Jing*, probably around 100BC, that *The Divine Husbandman's Classic of Herbal Medicine (Shen Nong Ben Cao Jing)* was published — the Divine Husbandman being Shen Nong, who probably died around three millenia earlier. It listed 365 herbs and their curative properties, tastes and energies and again was supposed to be based on the wisdom of the legendary emperor Shen Nong.

— Herbal knowledge, based on empirical research, grew in a more or less continuous manner over the following centuries. During this time many more herbals were written, each including an increasing number of herbs until, by the 16th century AD, there were nearly 2000 listed.

— After Western medicine began to penetrate China, traditional medicine went into a decline until it was resurrected by Chairman Mao. Today, it flourishes in China alongside Western medicine and its influence is simultaneously growing in the West as more of its philosophy and practice are understood.

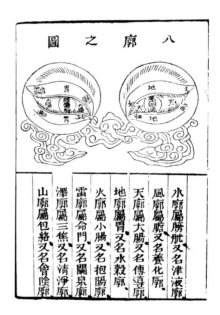

Above and detail left: *Chinese herbal medicine text written and illustrated by Tsung Chin Chien in the 18th-century.*

八廓之圖

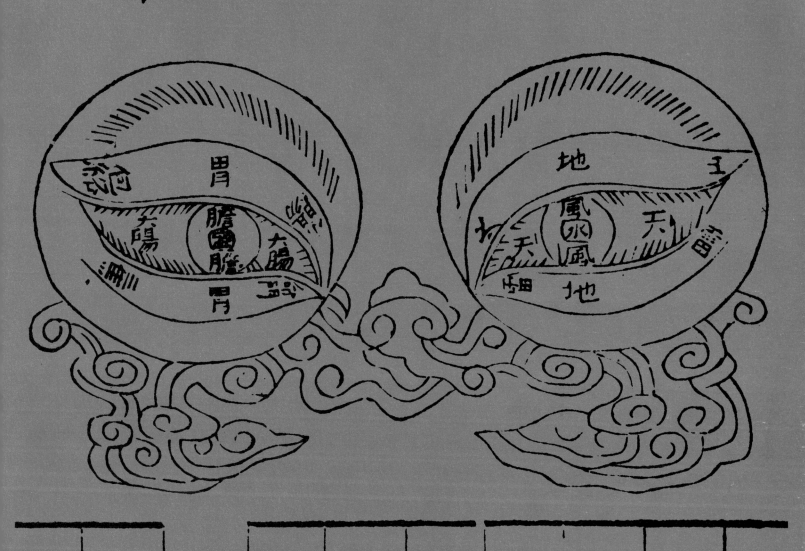

山廓屬包絡
澤廓屬三焦
雷廓屬命門
火廓屬小腸
地廓屬胃又
天廓屬大腸
風廓屬膽又
水廓屬膀胱

The Philosophy of Chinese Medicine

- After the era of prehistory when medicine in general and herbalism in particular were in the domain of shamans and emperors, they passed naturally into the hands of monks. Both Buddhism and Daoism had a great influence on Chinese thought and culture. Monks were often doctors and herbalists – as well as astronomers and calligraphers. Many were hermits, too, living alone in mountain caves where they would be visited by sick people hoping for a cure. Over the centuries, the knowledge of herbs and the understanding of the workings of the human body grew and became more formalized.

- As the organs of the body were discovered, they were deemed to be yin or yang. Yang organs are vital and solid and include the heart, spleen, lungs, kidneys and liver. Yang organs are hollow and functional and include the small and large intestines, the stomach, the bladder and the gall bladder. Each organ, however, also has a yin and yang element within it and it is the imbalance between them that leads to disease.

- Many ailments are defined in Chinese medicine as yin and yang. If someone is suffering from a yang deficiency, he will feel cold, both in himself and to the touch, and be pale and lethargic. He will often have a pale, swollen tongue and a weak pulse. The yin deficient person, on the other hand, may be hot or feverish, restless and in a state of constant stress. He will have a rapid pulse, a red face and a red tongue, perhaps with an unhealthy coating.

- The organs of the body, and the emotions and senses, are related to and governed by one of the elements, of which there are five in Chinese philosophy. First used in the study of astrology, the elements were adapted for medical use to explain the relationship between the internal organs and the properties of herbs and are fundamental to diagnosis and treatment. The Five Elements are wood, fire, earth, metal and water and they represent the endless circle of Life: Wood feeds fire. When it is burnt it nourishes and mingles with the earth. The earth creates metal and when metal becomes molten it resembles water. This water nourishes the trees, which give us wood.

Wood

- Wood signifies beginnings, creativity and expression. Expansive and unfolding, it governs both its yang organ, which is the the gall bladder, and its yin organ which is the liver.
- An excess of the wood element will result in anger and frustration. Someone suffering from this imbalance may have an inflexible and stiff body, taut muscles and a tendency to shout.
- A deficiency of wood, however, often leads to being timid and repressed, with no ability to express oneself. The patient may become depressed and cry easily and often has sore, red, itchy eyes and weak, ridged nails.
- Water feeds wood and wood feeds fire, according to the theory of the Five Elements. So anger, the emotion of wood, will be increased by fear, the emotion of water. An excess of wood, however, will stifle joy, the fire emotion.
- The taste associated with wood is sourness and so those suffering from a wood deficiency are likely to be prescribed sour-tasting herbs.

Among bamboos serene I sit alone,
Playing on the lyre and singing a high-pitched song.
In the thick woods no one will ever know of my presence;
The moon alone sends forth its lustrous rays.
Tu Fu (712–770AD)

The peace of a woodland setting was regarded as an ideal place for meditation. Here, the Seven Sages of the Bamboo Grove are depicted by Fu Pao-Shih (1904–65).

Fire

— The properties of fire are to warm and to blaze. Fire is linked to the mind and spirit. Its yang organs are the triple heater and the small intestine; its yin organs are the heart and pericardium.

— A fire imbalance can cause a whole range of emotional or psychological problems, including neurosis and schizophrenia. In less extreme cases there may be an unnaturally easy-going attitude if there is an excess, or an overly pessimistic one in the case of a deficiency. Physically, the imbalance may be inclined to manifest itself in palpitations or in excessive sweating. Fire is linked to speech and a deficiency may result in stammering or other speech impediments. If you have a fire-type constitution, you are likely to have red cheeks, bright eyes and an outgoing, cheerful personality.

— In Chinese medicine, fire is the element of joy and psychic energy. Its organ, the heart, is regarded as the house of both mind and spirit. It is assigned bitterness as its taste, so bitter herbs will be prescribed for a deficiency.

Below: *A dragon chases a flaming pearl – an exquisite detail from the base of a late 19th-century silver jardinière.*
Right: *The Blue Dragon Robe, the official costume of the Chinese Imperial Family and their bureaucrats.*

Visitors who call on a cold night
Are served tea instead of wine.
No sooner does the stove burst into flame
Then the water starts to bubble.
The same moon that shines in the heavens
In front of the window offers
A wholly different spectacle
After the first plum blossoms.
Tu Xiao-Shan (Sung period 960–1127AD)

Earth

- The properties of earth are to give, to receive and to concentrate. Its yang organ is the stomach and its yin organ the spleen.
- Those with an earth deficiency are often pale with dry, cracked lips and a tendency to plumpness, partly due to a craving for sweets. They may also suffer from poor digestion and weak muscles. Those with an earth deficiency tend to become indecisive and overdependent on others. A deficiency may also manifest itself in a toneless voice, whereas an excess gives speech a singsong quality. Those with an excess of the earth element are also inclined to be constant worriers.
- An excess of earth will overpower the next element in the cycle, metal, causing digestive problems. The taste related to earth is sweetness and small quantities of sweet herbs will restore a deficiency.

Casually I placed myself beneath the pines;
High on a stony pillow I lay down to sleep.
There is no calendar in these high mountains;
The winter ends, with no clear signs
To mark the year's changes.
Chui Lu (9th century)

From the days of shamans in caves and hermit monks, mountains became an outward expression of serenity and enlightenment. This early 18th-century portrait by the artist Yu Zhiding shows the scholar-official Han Yan deep in thought.

Metal

— Metal purifies, regulates and eliminates. Its yang organ is the large intestine, its yin organ, the lungs.

— Those with a metal imbalance may have respiratory problems and a tendency to colds and flu. A deficiency can often be observed in shortness of breath, wheeziness, a weak, sometimes whining voice, dry unhealthy skin and hair, constipation and general weakness. An excess will result in feverish energy and possibly an over sensitive sense of smell, a tendency to loose bowels and excessive body hair.

— Metal is the emotion of deep sadness and grief. It is associated with pungent tastes and herbs.

There came a sudden strain of music
Like a silver pitcher burst open,
With water gushing forth –
Like iron-clad horsemen sallying forth
With clashing swords and thudding spears.
Ending the song, she struck the centre of the lute;
Four strings, all plucked at once,
Sounded like a piece of silk being rent.
Po Zhuyi (9th century)

This 18th-century painting shows a group of musicians in the emperor's palace playing traditional instruments, including the classical Chinese lute and a half-tube zither.

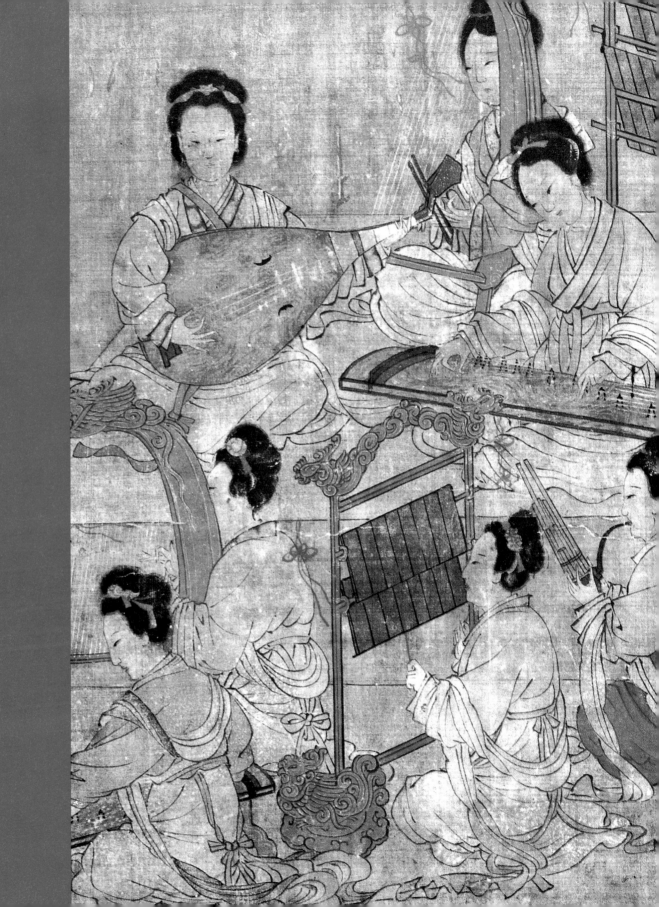

Water

- Water nourishes and is linked to power and the will. Its yang organ is the bladder and its yin organ is the kidneys.
- The water element is associated with the constitution we inherit, particularly with reference to growth, fertility and sexuality. A deficiency often leads to general weakness and fatigue, irregular menstruation, low sexual energy, impotence and infertility. It can make sufferers feel inadequate and fearful. Allied symptoms include asthma, loose teeth, thin hair, constipation, incontinence and poor hearing. An excess of water leads to overactive libido, seminal emission, premature ejaculation and sweating.
- Salty herbs, particularly seaweed, are often used to correct water deficiencies.

The lake in spring is like a picture;
Its level surface surrounded on all sides with the mountains,
Whose pines unfold their rows of green.
Like a pearl the moon's reflection shines in the lake
Early rice buds emerge like threads in a green blanket;
Like blue gauze skirt belts the young rushes extend.
Hangchow holds me; I cannot take leave of it,
And half the reason is this lake's beauty.
Po Zhuyi (772–846AD)

Water is a favourite subject for Chinese landscape painters.
It is also the element linked to Winter and cold, as portrayed
in this boating picture by Fu Pao-Shi (1904–65).

The External Causes of Disease

— According to Chinese pathology, there are three principal causes of the disharmony that brings about disease: external factors, emotions and irregularities in day-to-day living.

— External causes embrace a range of environmental conditions: wind, cold, fire, dryness, dampness and summer heat.

— Wind causes movement and change. It invades the body to cause dizziness, twitching, stiffness and convulsions. When combined with cold, it engenders colds, chills, flu and fever. It is related to the liver and can cause epilepsy and stroke. Its effects are thought to be strongest in the Spring.

— Cold constrains movement and warmth, often leading to stagnation. As well as possibly causing colds and chills when combined with wind, it can affect the lungs, resulting in expectorated mucus, and also the stomach and spleen, leading to vomiting or diarrhoea.

— Fire dries and its associated ailments include fevers, inflammations, constipation and infrequent urination. Psychologically, it results in irritability, lack of concentration, delirium and manic behaviour. In children it can sometimes result in hyperactivity.

— Dryness has a similar action to fire but with a tendency to dry body fluids. Symptoms include dry skin, cracked lips, a persistent cough with no phlegm and constipation.

— Dampness brings feelings of heaviness and sluggishness. Typical symptoms include headaches, lethargy, bloating, nausea and stiff, swollen and aching joints.

— Summer heat causes heatstroke, exhaustion and dehydration. It can result in fever and nausea.

Above and left: *Climate is one of the underlying causes of disease, according to traditional Chinese medicine. In keeping with the desire for moderation in all things, this pair of early 19th-century pictures shows travellers well wrapped against the Winter cold and a shady spot for a Summer fishing trip.*

The Internal Causes of Disease

- The importance of a balanced state extends to the emotions and mind as well as the body. An excess or a lack of emotional expression can lead to a disharmony that will manifest itself in both emotional and physical symptoms. No particular emotion is regarded as good or bad – any imbalance is seen as a potential cause of illness.

- Joy in excess leads to overexcitement or agitation, injury to the heart, insomnia, palpitations and hysteria.

- Anger causes resentment, frustration, rage and bitterness, injury to the liver, headaches, high blood pressure, menstrual problems and ailments of the stomach or spleen.

- Sadness affects the lungs and the heart and also causes breathlessness, fatigue, lowered immunity and insomnia.

- Pensiveness is caused by mental overwork or intellectual overstimulation and may lead to obsessiveness. It affects the spleen and also causes poor concentration, lethargy, loss of appetite and anaemia.

- Fear affects the kidneys, causing incontinence in adults and bed-wetting in children. It also reduces fertility, libido and general immunity to infection.

- Shock affects the kidneys and the heart. Imbalances also lead to palpitations, insomnia and fatigue.

Emotions can be a direct cause of ailments, according to traditional Chinese medicine. Pensiveness, sometimes also referred to as melancholy, is believed to lower immunity to disease. This melancholic early 16th-century illustration by Tang Yin depicts the Immortal Ge Changgeng.

The Lifestyle Causes of Disease

— The Chinese desire for balance in all things naturally includes the way we live our lives. Again, excesses or deficits are seen as generators of disease.

— Diet is very important in traditional Chinese medicine. A good diet is the foundation of good health and many ailments are cured simply by addressing basic nutritional imbalances. The ideal Chinese diet comprises food which is slightly warm to slightly cool in energy, such as fish, chicken, pork, beef, grains, cooked vegetables and certain fruits. Certain hot foods, especially fried foods, and drinks such as coffee, tea, chocolate, as well as cold foods, including salads and frozen foods like ice cream, should be taken in very limited amounts. Salt, sugar, caffeine and alcohol are regarded as toxins.

— Exercise supports the flow of energy. Without it, the Qi will stagnate. Excessive exercise, however, will lead to lowered immunity. In Chinese terms, exercise takes the form of techniques such as Tai Qi and Qi Gong, which focus on balance and concentration, the movements of the body being informed by both mind and spirit. Energetic exercise, for example aerobic exercise, has no role to play in the Chinese philosophy.

— Excessive libido and repeated childbirth can damage the health by sapping Qi energy. They can also result in lower back pain and failing hearing and eyesight.

This charming 18th-century portrait of lovers is one of an album of 12 erotic paintings. Too much sexual activity, however, is considered to have a deleterious effect on the health. Taoist yoga – in which there is sexual activity that never reaches a climax – is thought to prolong life and promote health.

Patterns of Disharmony

— Disharmony may be caused by external and internal factors or the excesses and deficiencies of an unbalanced lifestyle. Depending on the nature of the root cause, a pattern of disharmony is set up within the body and mind. It is the diagnosis of this underlying pattern that is the basis of the Chinese physician's treatment.

— There are numerous patterns of disharmony, many of which overlap, but most Chinese herbalists work from approximately 75 patterns, with innumerable further variations on these. The patterns themselves rest upon the Eight Principles: yin and yang, interior and exterior, cold and heat, deficiency and excess.

— Yin and yang make up the basic guiding principle for diagnosis. Yang embraces exterior, heat and symptoms and conditions related to excess. Yin embraces interior, cold and symptoms and conditions related to deficiency. There are four potent imbalances: yang excess exhibits itself in fever, impatience, bad temper, headaches, rapid pulse and high blood pressure. Yang deficiency often shows itself in night sweats, exhaustion, constipation, backache and impotence. Yin excess, which is very rarely seen, manifests itself in lethargy, aches, shivering, fluid retention and excessive mucus occurring in the lungs and nasal passages, in the bowel and as a vaginal discharge. Yin deficiency is exhibited in nervous exhaustion and tension, hot flushes and fevers.

— The words 'interior' and 'exterior' refer to the location of the ailment. Exterior conditions are caused by external factors and affect the skin, nose, mouth and hair. Symptoms include colds and fevers, injuries, sweating and skin problems. They are usually mild and often relieved by inducing sweating. Interior conditions are more severe and are usually caused by emotional and lifestyle factors. There is a range of symptoms, depending on the organ affected, including constipation, diabetes, infertility, impotence, lowered energy and heart problems. Treatment depends upon which organ is affected.

Climate is an important external factor that can cause disease. This 19th-century Taoist weather manual depicts fire (yang) and cloud (yin).

欻火會雷霆大煞雷震大作折樹誅妖驟雨傾盆

- 'Cold' and 'heat' identify the nature of the illness. Cold ailments lower the metabolism. Symptoms include an aversion to cold, pallor, slow pulse and slow movements, loose bowels and clear urine. Hot ailments overstimulate the metabolism and reveal themselves in fever, thirst, fast pulse and high blood pressure, dark urine and constipation, inflammation and aggressive behaviour.

- 'Deficiency' and 'excess' determine the body's Qi and resilience to the illness. Deficient Qi can be seen in general weakness, lack of immunity and emotional fragility. Excess Qi produces fever, infection, constipation and fluid retention.

- The Eight Principles combine into various patterns of disharmony and attach themselves to a particular organ or substance, as defined in traditional Chinese medicine. The principal organs are the heart, liver, lungs, spleen and kidneys. The substances are Shen, Qi, Jing, Blood and Body fluids.

Below: The eternally fluctuating balance of life is symbolized in the circular depiction of yin and yang.
Right: A 19th-century badge from the robe of a court official is embroidered with a dragon, the symbol of fertilizing rain, who would be approached to avert both drought and flood.

The Five Substances

— The Five Substances in traditional Chinese medicine embrace not only visible and tangible elements within the body, such as blood, but intangible ones, such as energy and spirit. The Five Substances are Shen, Qi, Jing, Blood and Body fluids.

— Shen is both 'mind' and 'spirit'. In Chinese medicine, it is based in the heart and governs memory and consciousness. It reflects spiritual, mental and emotional health. Symptoms associated with Shen imbalance are of the mind. A Shen deficiency reveals itself in lethargy, depression and insomnia. Excessive Shen results in anxiety, disturbing dreams and irrational behaviour. In extreme cases it can result in mania and schizophrenia. When Shen is in balance it provides a love of life and can be seen, quite literally, as a sparkle in the eyes.

— Qi is usually translated as 'energy', although it embraces more than mere physical vitality. The term 'life force' is closer to the Chinese understanding of Qi. It has various functions: moving in the sense of all bodily functions, both conscious and unconscious; transforming food and drink into energy; holding organs and other substances in their proper places. One cannot suffer from an excess of Qi. However, a Qi deficiency will lead to tiredness, poor appetite, slow recovery, weakness and palpitations. The other Qi imbalance is not an excess but a stagnation. This occurs when its flow through the body is irregular or blocked, either as a result of physical injury or an emotional blockage – frustration or stress, for example – that will show itself in lumps, indigestion and irritability.

Dreaming of Immortality by T'ang Yin (1470–1523) is a painting that attempts to embody Shen, the substance of mind and spirit.

爆竹生花

王承勳 圖

— Jing may be translated as 'essence' and refers to the fundamental nature of our constitution, in terms both of genetic inheritance and the way our lifestyle contributes to, or detracts from, our basic vitality. It governs fertility, sexuality and growth and is believed to have cycles during which development or decay takes place. For women, the cycles take place over seven years, but for men they last eight years.

— The cycles include growth of teeth and hair, puberty, the onset of menstruation, fertility, then later loss of teeth and hair, infertility and decrease of sexual fluids and finally the slowing down of the brain. It has only one imbalance, deficiency, to which men are more prone than women. In children it shows itself as slow mental and physical development, in adults as greying hair, brittle bones, low libido and wasting flesh.

— Blood includes the Western understanding of the blood that flows through our veins, but it is broadened into a much wider role of nourishing, warming and moistening, as well as having an interdependent relationship with both Shen and Qi. There are three imbalances. Deficiency can be seen in a pale face, tongue and lips, numbness, tremor and lightheadedness, scant periods and emaciation. Stagnations result in severe, stabbing pains, menstrual clots, purple nails and purple lips and tongue. Excessive heat in the blood may be due to toxins that cause fever and rashes.

— Body fluids include saliva, gastric juices, urine, tears and cerebrospinal and joint fluids. Deficient body fluids result in dryness in the lips, skin and hair, a dry cough and thirst. An excess causes oedema and an exhorbitant amount of any number of the body's fluids, such as phlegm, weeping skin rashes and vaginal discharge.

A family celebrates the New Year with fireworks in honour of the Kitchen God. Inherited family traits are part of the substance of Jing, or essence, which is also closely connected with the cycles of growth and ageing.

The Five Organs

— In traditional Chinese medicine the organs have an interdependent relationship with the Five Substances, being their creators, storers and nourishers. They are also considered to be closely related to specific emotions, which can be both positive and negative or vices and virtues. They have their own specific, essential needs which, if unfulfilled, will lead to imbalance and ill health.

— The heart governs the blood and blood vessels and also houses the Shen. For balance to be achieved, the heart needs love and the appreciation of beauty. When there is an imbalance, heart and circulation problems result, as well as insomnia and excessive nervous energy. Its associated negative emotion is overexcitement and its positive emotion is compassion.

— The lungs relate to the Qi and problems surface as susceptibility to colds, shallow, irregular breathing, coughs, asthma and shortness of breath. Lungs require confidence to be at their best. The associated negative emotion is sadness and its virtue is conscientiousness.

— The liver ensures that the Qi flows smoothly. An imbalance in the liver can cause all manner of problems from irregular periods to bad temper. The liver needs relaxation – and herbs – to function well. Its associated vice is anger and its virtue is benevolence.

— The spleen actually creates the Qi, as well as being the transformer of food into energy. Spleen imbalances are often due to a bad diet or mental stress and manifest themselves as poor appetite and loose stools. Good nutrition is essential for the spleen. Its associated vice is obsession and its virtue is empathy.

— The kidneys store the Jing and govern long-term growth and reproduction. Deficiency manifests itself in pallor, lassitude, infertility, oedema and diarrhoea. The kidneys need quiet, meditation and water to be in balance. Their negative emotion is fear and their positive emotions are courage and wisdom.

Kuan Yin, Goddess of Compassion, the ruling emotion of the heart.
Compassion is the supreme emotion of Buddhism, and
enlightenment brings with it total compassion for all living things.

Diagnosis
and Treatment

– The consultation and diagnosis given by a Chinese herbalist practitioner is likely to be similar to that given by an acupuncturist except that you do not need to undress. Chinese herbalist consulting rooms sometimes share clinic space with a herbal dispensary, which can look a bit like an old fashioned pharmacy, and your herbal prescription would normally be dispensed from here as you leave. Other practitioners, however, dispense the herbs themselves. The consulting room itself will probably be equipped for both acupuncture treatment and herbal prescribing. When you enter the consulting room the practitioner will immediately begin his looking examination, probably without you realizing it.

– Traditional Chinese medicine has to weigh up many factors and influences – yin and yang, the Five Elements, the Eight Principles, the various external and internal causes of disease, organs and substances – to discover the highly specific pattern, or patterns, of disharmony from which a patient may be suffering. Five methods of diagnosis are used: questioning, looking, smelling, listening and touching.

The Five Methods of Diagnosis

— A Chinese medical practitioner will usually want to ask you a lot of questions, especially on a first visit. These questions may not seem to a Western patient to be particularly relevant to the ailment, but as the practitioner will be searching for clues to your underlying pattern of disharmony, his questions will need to be very wide-ranging.

— Questions will include not only ones referring directly to your complaint but also to its development. Others will be to do with your diet and lifestyle, including which foods and drinks you prefer and whether you ever feel extreme hunger or thirst, the nature and frequency of your urination and bowel movements, difficulties in menstruation, intercourse or fertility, whether you are prone to chills or fevers, how often and how much you perspire, whether you suffer from general aches and pains, including whether you have frequent headaches or back pain. You may be asked about your childhood and family, dreams and sleep patterns, your emotional life and your response to different climates or your energy pattern as it changes during the course of a typical day.

— Observation is a vital part of diagnosis in Chinese medicine. This takes in the outward appearance of strength and health, or lack of it. Vitality, whether you have sluggish movements or jerky ones, is relevant and whether you seem calm or nervous and are easily startled. The skin, face and hair all give clues to the nature of your ailment. Bags under the eyes, for example, indicate a kidney imbalance, a red face suggests excessive heat, while red, swollen eyes indicate a liver problem.

— The tongue is examined in terms of its colour, shape, size and texture. A pale tongue indicates a deficiency of Qi and blood, whereas a purple one suggests blood stagnation. A swollen tongue indicates that the spleen is yang deficient, while one with cracked edges suggests that the spleen is Qi deficient.

— The coating on the tongue also gives important diagnostic information. Normally, the tongue has a thin, white coating that is easy to remove. However, if the coating is grey, there is probably a yin deficiency and an excess of fire. A bright red tongue with little or no coating indicates a yin deficiency.

— While inspecting the tongue, the practitioner will generally smell the breath and body odour, as this may indicate particular imbalances. He may also ask you about the smell of your urine or stools.

— The quality of the voice is another diagnostic indicator, with special relevance to the lungs, heart and voice. The pitch, whether it is loud or faint, and the evenness or otherwise of the breathing may all suggest particular imbalances.

The traditional Chinese physician begins his diagnosis with careful and extensive questioning. At the same time, he observes his patient closely as he answers, as much can be discovered from tone of voice as from the answers themselves.

- Touch is the most important of the diagnostic tools and takes two forms – palpating and pulse taking.
- Palpation is the manual feeling of the body. It includes feeling the patient's temperature: it is possible for a patient to feel chilled although the surface of his skin is hot to the touch. The moisture content in the skin may be relevant: clammy skin, for example, often indicates a lung imbalance. Finally, by gently palpating along the meridians, the practitioner can search for areas of tenderness, and hence, blockages.
- Pulse taking is one of the most fundamental Chinese diagnostic practices – as well as being perceived as one of the most controversial by the West. In Western medicine the pulse is also taken routinely but in traditional Chinese medicine there are 12 pulses to take, not one. Within these 12 pulses there are a full complement of 28 pulse qualities. The taking of the pulses is considered to be a specialized art, and requires a great deal of practice and sensitivity.
- There are three pulse locations on each wrist, each of which is felt with light and then heavy pressure. The three pulses on the left wrist relate to the heart, small intestine, liver, bladder, gall bladder and kidney yin. On the right wrist, the three pulses indicate the health of the lungs, large intestine, spleen, stomach, pericardium, triple heater and kidney yang.
- Abnormality of pulses takes various forms. A feeble pulse indicates a Qi or Blood deficiency, while an over-vigorous one often predicts the onset of an illness. When making a diagnosis a practitioner must consider not only the rhythm of the pulse but also its depth and strength.

Above: *Pulse taking is perhaps the most important of all diagnostic methods used in traditional Chinese medicine. This 19th-century watercolour shows a physician taking the pulse of his female patient.*
Right: *Sometimes, as here, the simplest observation can reveal the source of an ailment!*

左脇肝氣痛

氣虛背痛

右脇肺氣痛

必腹痛

心氣痛

The bark of the cherry tree (Prunus yedoensis or Ying pi) is sometimes used as a means of detoxification. A pair of birds on a cherry tree are depicted in this piece of 20th-century Chinese hand embroidery.

How Herbs Are Used

— The herbs are classified according to their basic actions — by what they do rather than what they are. Among the 20 groups within this system there are classifications for easing rheumatism, regulating energy, reducing anxiety and treating ulcers and tumours.

— Herbs and their cultivation are a major industry in parts of China, although some herbs are only considered efficacious when found growing in their natural environment. Many plants are used for different remedies, according to which part of the plant is utilized. The time to harvest depends upon whether the roots are needed — dug out in late autumn or early spring, or the leaves — picked before the flowers bloom or the flowers themselves, which are picked while still in bud.

— Correct processing of the herb is essential. Alcohol, honey, vinegar or salt may be used and the plant may also be heated or moistened to release its curative properties. This processing can change the character of a plant, notably in the case of poisonous plants — such as camphor, opium poppy, nightshade or black false hellebore — which are rendered into a form where they can be taken safely.

— Chinese herbs are not necessarily herbs as we know them. Besides the common Western herbs, the Chinese also use tuberous roots, grains, seeds, tree bark and the stems, flowers and fruits of various plants, as well as their leaves. More surprisingly, they also include minerals, such as gypsum, alum and clay, and a wide range of different animal parts, as diverse as oyster shells, fossilized bones, leeches, dried cicadas and donkey skin.

— According to legend, the Yellow Emperor started compiling a list of Chinese medicinal herbs in about 3000BC. The listing of herbs and their properties continued over the centuries, and there are now thousands whose curative properties are known, and huge numbers of these that are still available and in common use.

This delicate watercolour on silk depicts a bunch of flowers. The root of the distinctive, bright blue Chinese Gentian is used to reduce swelling and soreness, particularly of the eyes, ears or throat. It can also be used for digestive problems and for an analgesic.

The Five Tastes

— Chinese herbs are considered to have a specific taste. There are five tastes: sweet, bitter, pungent, salty and sour. These tastes reflect the healing function of particular herbs and the organs of the body that they affect. A herb can have more than one taste — including sweet and bitter together — and this can be a confusing concept for Western palates. Quantity is important, too, and while an appropriate amount of a given herb will cure an ailment, an excess of the same herb will make the condition worse.

— Sweet herbs warm, harmonize, moderate, relax and act as a tonic. They particularly affect the spleen and the stomach and strengthen people who feel weak or whose energy is impaired. Sweetness in terms of Chinese herbalism is not the obvious sweetness of refined sugar. Common sweet-tasting herbs include cinnamon, licorice, bamboo shoots and ginseng.

— Bitter herbs detoxify, dry, cool and disperse and are closely linked to both the heart and small intestine. They act on diarrhoea and skin abscesses, cleanse the blood and protect against parasites. Bitter herbs include watercress, gentian and rhubarb.

— Pungent herbs are sometimes referred to as acrid or spicy and their prime action is to stimulate. They act particularly on the lungs and large intestine and increase energy and invigorate the circulation and digestion. Because they tend to open the pores and encourage sweating, they are beneficial for colds and flu. Ginger, mint and black pepper are typical pungent herbs.

— Salty herbs concentrate and soften, and specifically affect the kidneys and bladder. The softening effect is beneficial for hardened lymph nodes, cysts, tight muscles and constipation. Seaweed typifies salty herbs.

— Sour herbs affect the liver and gall bladder and their action is to absorb, contract and refresh. They are beneficial in stopping diarrhoea, excessive perspiration, bleeding and seminal emission. They also stimulate the digestion. Sour herbs include lemon, crab apple, orange peel and gooseberry.

The Five Energies

— In addition to the various tastes, herbs are also assigned a particular energy. They can be hot, warm, neutral, cool or cold. The two extremes of hot and cold are used less often than the gentler actions of warm and cool. Neutral energy is balanced.

— Hot herbs such as aconite or ginger and warm herbs such as angelica, epimedium and cnidium (the latter two being aphrodisiacs), are used for ailments with a yang deficiency. They warm and stimulate the body and increase energy.

— Cold herbs such as the Chinese white rose *(Cynanchum atratum)*, artemisia and honeysuckle and cool herbs such as peony root, mint and forsythia slow the metabolism and clear the heat of fever or infection, reducing overactive yang energy.

— Neutral energy neither warms nor cools. Neutral herbs include reishi and mistletoe.

— Herbs are also deemed to have one of four directions. Rising herbs such as black pepper take the energy upwards and invigorate the circulation. Sinking herbs such as angelica take the energy down and can calm the mind as well as activating the bowels and the bladder. Outward energy in a herb such as peppermint induces sweating and acts on colds and flu. Inward energy strengthens the organs, ginseng being a particularly effective example.

Honeysuckle – a cold herb used to reduce fever – is depicted in this late 19th-century painting on silk.

How to Take Herbs

— Chinese herbs can be taken in many different ways. The simplest is as a tea, usually made from dried herbs. The herbs are left to infuse for 10 to 20 minutes in boiling water. The dried herbs can also be decocted. To do this the herbs are simmered in water for 20 to 30 minutes, after which the liquid is strained before drinking.

— Powders are ground herbs or those that have been decocted and then dried into a more concentrated form. Usually, the powder is mixed in warm water before drinking, although sometimes it is given in capsule form. Powders can also be used for external application. They are mixed with oil or water before being applied to the skin. Granules are a modern variation on powders.

— Tinctures are made by soaking herbs in alcohol — red wine is preferred for women as it replenishes the blood after menstruation. They are considered an effective form for herbs used to stimulate energy and circulation.

— Liniments are prepared in the same way as tinctures but are applied externally to treat injuries and ease muscular aches and pains.

— Pills are usually made in China and exported. They are absorbed more slowly than teas, powders and tinctures and so are ideal for conditions that require prolonged, slow release of the prescription.

— Congees are a kind of soup in which herbs are cooked with rice until they turn into a thick porridge. They are extremely nutritious and therefore particularly appropriate for convalescents or patients with debilitating diseases.

The Chinese ladies in this 19th-century painting are shown enjoying the pleasures of their garden while drinking tea. Tea is the simplest way to prepare therapeutic herbs.

Combinations and Formulae

— Herbalists rarely prescribe a single herb. Instead, a combination, in which the balance between individual herbs brings about a particular curative effect, is used. Within the formula the herbs are ascribed a 'rank', according to their relative importance and strength. In descending order they are Jun (emperor), Chen (minister), Zuo (assistant) and Shi (messenger). There are age-old traditional recipes still in use for such treatments as strengthening the Qi, nourishing the blood and curing colds and fevers.

— The most popular of these formulae are available as Chinese herbal patent medicines. In parts of China, whole villages work on growing and processing the herbs that make up particular patents. Having been in use for hundreds, often thousands, of years, the patent formulae are known to have no side effects and are usually available as pills.

The growing and preparation of herbs for medicinal use is an important part of Chinese agriculture. In this 13th or 14th-century painting attributed to Cheng Chi, rice – used as a base for congees in Chinese nutritional therapy – is threshed and winnowed by peasants.

A Selection
of Chinese Herbs

— There are thousands of Chinese herbs and hundreds still in common use. In a book of this size, only a small selection of these herbs can be covered. However, it will serve to show the enormous scope of ailments that can be relieved by the use of Chinese herbs and the equally vast range of ailments for which an individual herb can be used, depending on the circumstances.

— The legends that follow illustrate the accidental method by which many herbal remedies were discovered. The stories are rather like fairy tales – they include perhaps a very small grain of historical fact – but their main purpose is a means of remembering herb lore. Some legends are thought to predate written language, and they form part of an oral tradition in which the essential knowledge of herbs and health could be passed on.

— Some of the herbs included will be familiar to Western readers. Ginseng, for example, although very much a Chinese herb, is now well known in the West. Others are plants that Westerners would not regard as herbs such as clematis and magnolia. Still others have Western cousins such as hawthorn and mistletoe, although sometimes those cousins are regarded as weeds – dandelion and plantain, for example.

— The wonder of Chinese herbal medicine is that over the centuries it has investigated virtually every element of its landscape in its search for the restoration of harmony which, according to its principles, is health.

Ginseng

Panax ginseng   **Ren Shen** (man's root)

— Energy and taste: slightly warm, sweet, slightly bitter

— Part used: root

— Uses: a tonic for the whole system, treating all deficiency diseases accompanied by symptoms such as chronic fatigue, insomnia, weakness, forgetfulness, breathlessness, diarrhoea, prolapse, tinnitus, impotence or palpitations with anxiety. Particularly recommended for the elderly and those who are convalescing after illness

— Contraindications: not to be used by those with high blood pressure. Eating turnips lessens its effect

Ginseng is a tonic to the five organs, quieting the animal spirits, stabilizing the soul, preventing fear, expelling the vicious energies, brightening the eye and improving vision, opening up the heart, benefitting the understanding and, if taken for some time, will invigorate the body and prolong life.

The Divine Husbandman

— Two brothers foolishly went out hunting in the mountains in the middle of Winter, though they were warned of the dangers. At first all went well and they killed many animals. Suddenly, the weather changed and the snow fell so hard that all the paths were blocked and they were trapped in the mountains with no food. Days went by and, in desperation, they began to eat the roots of the only plant they could find growing. By eating this, they survived. In fact, not only did they survive but, to their surprise, they found themselves remarkably healthy. In the spring, they returned to their village and everyone was astonished they were alive. They told of the roots they had eaten, explaining the strange shape they had – just like a man! This was how ginseng got its name, Ren Shen, or man's root.

A painting from the Ming period (1368–1644AD) of a Mongolian archer, his bow and arrows strapped to his elaborately decorated steed.

Chinese Hawthorn

Crataegus pinnatifida   **Shan Zha** (red berries)

— **Energy and taste:** slightly warm, sour, sweet
— **Part used:** fruit
— **Uses:** reduces indigestion, abdominal distension, wind, diarrhoea, dysentery, hypertension and hernia. Is regarded as a tonic for the heart and is thought to lower blood pressure
— **Contraindications:** weak digestion

— A boy was often left alone with his stepmother while his father was away. The stepmother resented the child and wanted to kill him — but without being found out. She devised a novel plan. She would feed him only on half-cooked rice and he would die of indigestion. After a few weeks of putting her plan into action, it seemed to be working and the boy grew thin and complained of stomach pains. Then, while he was out in the mountains, he picked some berries from a tree. Finding them delicious, he returned every day to eat more and grew strong and healthy. The wicked stepmother could not understand what had gone wrong and was so afraid that the child was being protected by a god that she gave up her evil plan altogether.

An interior of a Chinese house, from a book of Chinese watercolours (c. 1820–1840), showing a happier family scene than the one described in the legend of the Chinese hawthorn.

Licorice

Glycyrrhiza uralensis **Gan Cao** (sweet grass)

— Energy and taste: neutral, sweet
— Part used: root
— Uses: detoxifies, energizes, strengthens,
   relieves sore throats, coughing and wheezing,
   stomach and duodenal ulcers. Is thought to
   protect the liver and prevent flu
— Contraindications: nausea and vomiting,
   oedema, high blood pressure

— While her husband was away, a herbalist's wife decided to try
her hand at treating his patients. Knowing nothing at all of
herbalism, she decided to find the herb with the sweetest,
most pleasant taste and give it to all the patients, as they
would be sure to like it. Strangely, this policy worked well and
everyone felt much better, whatever their original ailment. On
his return, the herbalist investigated this remarkable herb
further and discovered it brought increased energy at the
same time as relieving pain. Its delicious taste gave it the
name 'sweet grass'.

*An oil painting dating from the mid 19th-century of a
Chinese garden with three ladies. Besides a wide variety
of plants – with both decorative and medicinal uses –
moving water was a highly desirable feature for a
garden, contributing good Qi.*

Japanese Honeysuckle

Lonicera japonica   **Jin Yin Hua** (gold-silver flower)

- Energy and taste: cold, sweet
- Part used: flower
- Uses: acute fevers, dysentery, sore throats, headaches
- Contraindications: diarrhoea

- There were once two beautiful twin sisters called Golden Flower and Silver Flower, who lived in a small village in China. Even as tiny children, they were devoted to each other and vowed they would never marry so that they could stay together forever. When they were 17, Golden Flower fell ill with a fever and red spots. The village doctor said the disease was not only incurable, it was also contagious and so nobody should go near her. But Silver Flower stayed with her sister in spite of all warnings. Within days, Silver Flower, too, was ill and the two girls died soon after and were buried in the same grave.

- The next spring, a new plant grew on their grave. It was covered with beautiful flowers with yellow and white petals. After the plant had blossomed, two little girls — another pair of twins — fell ill with the very same disease as Golden Flower and Silver Flower. Again, the doctor shook his head and said it was incurable. Their parents were distraught and, in desperation, made a drink for their daughters of the flowers of the new plant. To everyone's delight, the children recovered. A cure had been found and it was believed the new plant was the entwined spirits of Golden Flower and Silver Flower.

This delicate piece of 19th-century embroidery depicts two Chinese ladies in a garden. In the foreground is a peony, the root of which is used to treat anaemia, menstrual problems, headaches and dizziness.

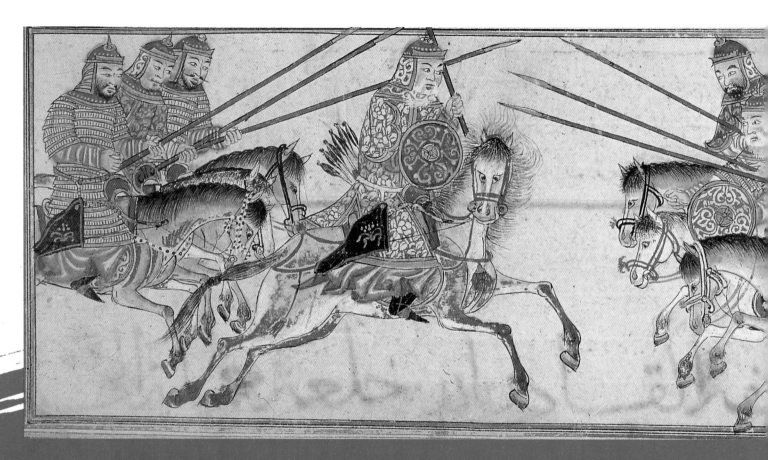

*This 13th-century illuminated manuscript depicts
a battle between rival Mongol tribes.*

Chinese Yam

Dioscorea opposita   **Shan Yao** (mountain medicine)

- Energy and taste: neutral, sweet
- Part used: root
- Uses: fatigue, poor appetite, diabetes, chronic diarrhoea, sweating, vaginal discharge, seminal emission, asthma, bronchitis, emphysema

- A long time ago there was a great battle that ended in a resounding victory. The defeated army escaped into a high mountain but their enemies surrounded its foot, trapping the fleeing army. The victors began to celebrate – their opponents would simply starve to death, they reasoned. A year went by but not a single soldier had surrendered. Then one night, a strong and fierce army came down from the mountain and overpowered the celebrating besiegers. Far from starving, they had found a plant with big roots that had made them stronger and more powerful than ever. They called it 'mountain medicine' after the place where they had found it growing.

Clematis

Clematis chinensis   **Wei Ling Xian** (temple's holy root)

— **Energy and taste:** warm, pungent, salty
— **Parts used:** root and stem
— **Uses:** arthritis, rheumatism, oedema,
jaundice and softening fish bones stuck
in the throat

— There was a Buddhist temple at the top of a high mountain in
China where many people came to worship. Most of these
people suffered from rheumatism and arthritis and were
treated by an old nun who lived at the temple. The old nun
gave them a herb soup but she pretended that it was a gift
from Buddha and contained no herbs at all. The treatment was
very successful and the people gave generous donations to
the temple. There was also a young nun in the temple who
decocted the herbs and was angry about the deceit. One day,
in order to expose the old nun, the young nun decided she
would prepare the wrong herbs and, of course, the patients,
far from improving, found that their illnesses got worse. The
young nun secretly gave them a new treatment she had
discovered and told them the truth about the herbs. When the
old nun discovered what had happened she became so angry
she had hysterics and died of a heart attack. The young nun
decided to give free treatment to the people and cured many
of rheumatism and arthritis with the herb she had discovered,
calling it 'temple's holy root'.

*Buddhist temples were often sited in remote
areas, as is the setting of this 'mountain
cottage' painted by Pu Ru (1896–1963).
High mountains and water were both
considered conducive to a life of the spirit.*

古樹鳴斜
照蒼蒼山起
暮雲
四山高

Two ladies in a room from a book of Chinese watercolours (1820–1840). Interestingly, even in this dark and gloomy interior, the Chinese love of plants and herbs is evident – both in paintings and growing in pots.

A Selection of Chinese Herbs

Boneset

Eupatorium fortunei **Pei Lan** (sister-in-law's orchid)

& Korean Mint

Agastache rugosa **Hua Xiang** (sister-in-law's mint)

— **Energy and taste:** Pei Lan – neutral,
pungent; Huo Xiang – slightly warm, pungent

— **Parts used:** Pei Lan – stalks and leaves;
Huo Xiang – leaves

— **Uses:** Pei Lan – relieves headache due to
Summer heat, inhibits flu; Huo Xiang –
relieves nausea, vomiting, diarrhoea,
morning sickness

— When a young man went off to the wars, his wife, Pei Lan, and
sister, Huo Xiang, decided to live together. They became great
friends, living in special harmony. One day, Pei Lan fell ill with
sunstroke and her sister-in-law put her to bed, then went to
the mountain to find herbs to cure her. Pei Lan implored her
not to go as there were so many dangers on the mountain, but
Huo Xiang insisted. Night fell and dawn came and still she did
not return. Then, late the next morning, she returned and
immediately collapsed on the floor, telling Pei Lan she'd been
bitten by a poisonous snake. Pei Lan climbed out of bed and
tried to suck the poison from the wound, but in vain. The two
women were discovered dead on the floor the next day by a
neighbour. Next to them were the two herbs gathered by Huo
Xiang that they had never had time to prepare. These now
bear their names.

Mistletoe

Loranthus parasiticus   **Sang Ji Sheng** (mulberry parasite)

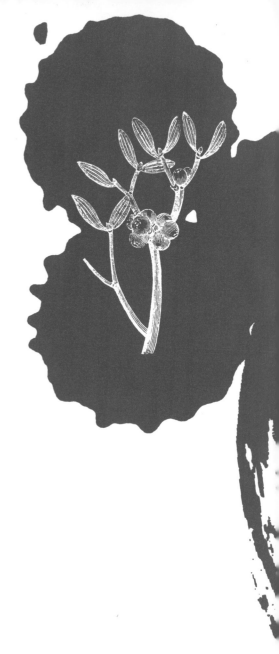

— Energy and taste: neutral, bitter

— Part used: stalks

— Uses: lumbago, weak legs, insecure foetus,
  shortage of milk in nursing mothers

— Note: the bark of the mulberry *(Morus alba)*
  is itself used for bronchitis, asthma, coughing
  and wheezing with phlegm

— A young man was so ill he had been bedridden for many years.
  His wealthy father, hearing of a renowned herbalist hundreds
  of miles away, sent his servant for a cure. The servant made
  numerous journeys and brought back many herbs, but the
  young man never improved. One day, the servant was on his
  way to the herbalist yet again, when it began to snow.
  Stopping to rest under a white mulberry tree, he noticed a
  herb growing on a branch. Intrigued, he picked the plant and
  decided to take it back to his wealthy master, pretending he
  had been to the herbalist. The ruse worked and so he
  continued to pick the same plant repeatedly to save himself
  the arduous journey. To his great surprise, his master's son
  improved. The servant confessed and the master was too
  delighted by his son's recovery to punish his servant for
  his deceit.

*An early 19th-century album painting of a rider
in a mountain landscape – a cold, bleak and
intensely yin scene.*

Magnolia

Magnolia liliflora   **Xin Yi Hua** (barbarian bud)

— Energy and taste: warm, pungent
— Part used: dried buds
— Uses: nasal discharge, sinusitis, headache
— Note: the magnolia bark *(Magnolia officinalis)* is used for digestive disorders

— A government official suffered so badly from a disease of the nose that he decided to retire early and go to live in seclusion in the country. While he was debating where he would live, he went on a tour to the frontier. There he met a herbalist who cured his disease and gave the official some seeds so he could grow the herb himself. He returned home and took up his work again, pointing out the herb growing in his garden as the 'barbarian bud' because it came from the frontier with the barbarians.

Above: A flowering magnolia tree appears in the foreground of this contemporary Chinese painting.
Right: The court was at the centre of Chinese life for many centuries and an official position was sought by every ambitious young man. The court itself was often magnificent, as shown in this 17th-century painting on silk of the Emperor Yang Di in his gardens with his wives.

Reishi

Ganoderma lucidum   **Ling Zhi** (spiritual vegetable meat)

– **Energy and taste:** neutral, bitter
– **Part used:** whole plant
– **Uses:** fatigue, cancer, tumours, heart disease, insomnia, stress

– A young man wanted to become a government official but, having failed the examinations, he decided to become a Taoist monk instead. Although he was very dedicated, he began to waste away until he was nothing but skin and bone. So he left the temple and went to the city, where he made a great fortune as a builder though he remained as thin as a wraith. One day one of his workers dug up a strange object from the ground that was soft and fleshy, like a human hand. Everyone was very frightened, believing it was a bad omen. The man sought the advice of a fortune teller, who said that the only way to avert disaster was for him to eat this strange object. The man was disgusted but he was also very afraid and so he agreed. A few days later he noticed he had put on weight, his grey hair had regained its original colour and he looked like a young man again.

– Some days afterwards, a Taoist monk passed by and, seeing his extraordinary transformation, examined him and asked him what he had eaten. When he described it, the monk explained to him that it was a mushroom called 'spiritual vegetable meat' and, having eaten it, he should leave the mundane world and concentrate on the spirit. The man was happy to return to the temple with the monk and become a monk once more.

Above: *The Ling Zhi fungus is held in the beak of a crane, companion to an Immortal in this 18th-century jade carving.*
Right: *A 19th-century painting of 'A Wandering Monk'. His accompanying tiger is a symbol of yang energy, but the monk's own aim would be to achieve a perfect balance of yin and yang energies.*

A Selection of Chinese Herbs

Asiatic Plantain

Plantago asiatica   **Che Qian Ren** (plant before the cart)

— Energy and taste: cold, sweet

— Part used: whole plant

— Uses: relieves dysentery, bleeding, blood in
the urine, nosebleeds, stings, bites and
soothes coughs and irritated eyes

— Ma-Wu was a great general of the Han dynasty
(206BC–220AD). Defeated in battle, he was forced to retreat
with his army to a part of the country where there was both
drought and famine. Men and horses were dying of thirst and
starvation and they all had a mysterious symptom – blood in
the urine. Ma-Wu was distraught when he saw the horses in
his charge also had blood in their urine but he could do nothing
to help them. One day Ma-Wu's groom noticed to his joy that
the horses' symptoms had cleared up. Watching them
carefully, he discovered that they were grazing on some low-
growing plants. He pulled some out and boiled them in water
and, when he drank it, his own symptoms disappeared. He
rushed to Ma-Wu who ordered all his soldiers and horses to
take the remedy. All were cured. Ma-Wu asked his groom
where he had found this wonderful plant and the groom told
him it was before the cart where he had taken the horses to
graze, so the general gave it that name.

Equestrian warriors parade around the border of a
large and unusual 18th-century **famille verte** *panel.*

Dandelion

Taraxacum mongolicum   **Pu Gong Ying** (fisherman's herb)

— **Energy and taste**: cold, bitter, sweet
— **Part used**: root
— **Uses**: breast abscesses, mastitis, urinary
infections, jaundice, red swollen eyes, fevers
and to encourage lactation
— **Note**: dandelion is high in vitamins A and C
as well as iron. The ground root is roasted
and made into 'coffee' for the elderly, sick
and children

— The young daughter of a high official discovered a lump in her
breast. This made her very frightened and ashamed. When her
father found out about her condition, he became very angry,
saying she must have done something immoral to have caused
it. The girl pleaded her innocence but to deaf ears and, in
despair, went to the river to take her life. As she jumped in, a
fisherman and his daughter saw her and rescued her. The two
girls were the same age and, as the fisherman's daughter
gave her new friend dry clothes, she saw the reason for her
despair. The fisherman said he knew of a herb to cure her, and
over the following days she drank a liquid from the herb and
applied a poultice of it to her breast. Her parents, filled with
remorse, sought her out and were amazed to discover that she
was cured. The fisherman gave her the herb to continue to
keep her well. She planted it in her garden and named it after
the fisherman, whose name she never knew.

*This pensive, well-dressed young lady looks out of
her window in a sumptuous 18th-century painting
by Lam Qua.*

Glossary

Chen	minister
Congee	a kind of soup or porridge made with rice and herbs and used for invalids
Jing	essence or inherited constitution
Jun	emperor
Nei Jing	Chinese herbal, written in the form of a discussion between the legendary Yellow Emperor and his physician, Chi Bo
Qi	the life force or energy
Qi Gong	a system of exercises designed to promote good health and protect against disease
Shen	mind or spirit
Shi	messenger
Tai Qi	a martial art with its roots in traditional Chinese medicine, that promotes the flow of Qi and balance within the body
Triple Heater	traditional term used to describe the three body cavities which comprise the chest, abdomen and lower abdomen
Yang	the male principle, representing positivity, activity, heat, light, vigour, day, Summer
Yin	the female principle, representing negativity, passivity, cold, dark, stillness, night, Winter
Zuo	assistant

Index

Acknowledgements

The publishers wish to thank the following organizations for their kind permission to reproduce the photographs in this book:

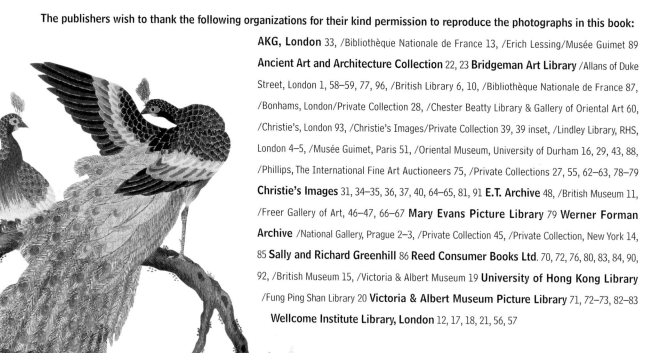

AKG, London 33, /Bibliothèque Nationale de France 13, /Erich Lessing/Musée Guimet 89 **Ancient Art and Architecture Collection** 22, 23 **Bridgeman Art Library** /Allans of Duke Street, London 1, 58–59, 77, 96, /British Library 6, 10, /Bibliothèque Nationale de France 87, /Bonhams, London/Private Collection 28, /Chester Beatty Library & Gallery of Oriental Art 60, /Christie's, London 93, /Christie's Images/Private Collection 39, 39 inset, /Lindley Library, RHS, London 4–5, /Musée Guimet, Paris 51, /Oriental Museum, University of Durham 16, 29, 43, 88, /Phillips, The International Fine Art Auctioneers 75, /Private Collections 27, 55, 62–63, 78–79 **Christie's Images** 31, 34–35, 36, 37, 40, 64–65, 81, 91 **E.T. Archive** 48, /British Museum 11, /Freer Gallery of Art, 46–47, 66–67 **Mary Evans Picture Library** 79 **Werner Forman Archive** /National Gallery, Prague 2–3, /Private Collection 45, /Private Collection, New York 14, 85 **Sally and Richard Greenhill** 86 **Reed Consumer Books Ltd.** 70, 72, 76, 80, 83, 84, 90, 92, /British Museum 15, /Victoria & Albert Museum 19 **University of Hong Kong Library** /Fung Ping Shan Library 20 **Victoria & Albert Museum Picture Library** 71, 72–73, 82–83 **Wellcome Institute Library, London** 12, 17, 18, 21, 56, 57

Publishing Director: **Laura Bamford**

Commissioning Editor: **Jane McIntosh**

Editors: **Catharine Davey**

Clare Hill

Arlene Sobel

Creative Director: **Keith Martin**

Senior Designer: **Geoff Fennell**

Picture Research: **Charlotte Deane**

Production Controller: **Julie Hadingham**

Herbalist Consultant: **Helen Fielding MRCHM**

Poetry excerpts are taken from *One Hundred and One Chinese Poems*, translated by Shih Shun Lui, Hong Kong University Press, 1967